MANHATTAN
A POEM

THOMAS FOGARTY

MANHATTAN

by
CHARLES HANSON TOWNE
author of "The Quiet Singer"

Charles Hanson Towne

Charles Hanson Towne was born in 1877; an author, poet, editor and popular celebrity, he spent most of his life in New York. Towne spent his early life in Kentucky however, moving to the city with his family at the age of three. He began his literary career remarkably early - at the age of eleven when he became the 'publisher' of the *Unique Monthly,* a children's magazine written by and for Towne and his friends. His first real job came with a position as editorial assistant at *Cosmopolitan* (originally a family magazine, and a literary journal during Towne's era). In 1901, Towne moved up the career ladder to *Smart Set,* a publication squarely aimed at sophisticated urban clients. He was remarkably successful with this company, and was appointed overall editor in 1904 - a trend which continued for the remainder of his career.

Towne also wrote many of his own much celebrated poems, plays, essays and novels - on various subjects surrounding life in New York City. Through this oeuvre, he quickly became known as the 'quintessential New Yorker', carrying on with his editorial duties at magazines such as *Delineator, Designer, McClure's and Harper's Bazaar.* Some of Towne's best known poems include: *Beyond the Stars,* a work which invites the reader not to fear death, but revel in its glory, *Around the Corner,* another poem which speaks of friendship and loss - yet hopes for 'tomorrow', and *Manhattan: A Poem,* speaking of his love of the great American city.

For almost the entire 1930s, Towne wrote a personal and literary column for the *New York American,* as well as making use of his fame in the poetry world, by teaching a poetry course at Columbia University. Towne was never a man to settle down though, and in 1940, joined the touring company of the Broadway show, *Life with Father.* His exploits have all been documented for posterity with his autobiography, *So Far, So Good.* Towne died in 1949, at the age of seventy-two. He left behind a vast amount of writing, still much renowned today.

MANHATTAN

I

ITY I love—and hate!—how can I sing
The miracle of your might in such a
mood?
How can I still the anger in my heart,
To tell of your great beauty? How dispel
The anguish I have known at your strong hands,
To whisper of your wonder? O City, how
Can I forget your loveliness, to sing
Ev'n for one hour your terror and despair?
Lo! I am of your children, and all day
Behind your granite walls, hemmed in by stone,
I struggle with my brothers, till my heart
Grows sick with sighing. Like some stricken bird,
Long since I beat upon my bars, and sought
Blessed release; but now—I only wait,
And dream, and hunger; and I sometimes think
If one should come to set my spirit free,
Would I go gladly?

MANHATTAN

            Nay, the chains are strong
That bind me to these paves; but stronger yet
The spiritual thraldom that I know—
The madness in the blood and in the brain
That comes and grows and flourishes, until
It is a very portion of ourselves,
And teaches us to lose our youthful dream
Of God's wide gardens and His quiet woods;
And tells us to forget the ancient truths,
The little paths which sundown used to paint
With all the gorgeous color of the world.
Lost peace! lost rapturous evenings! olden dawns!
When shall I feel again your healing kiss
Upon my tired eyes?
                Not lost indeed
Is your fresh beauty—only vanished now,
While I am prisoner here a little while.

I heard a quiet voice
   Call to my aching heart;
But I did not dare rejoice,
   Lest swift it should depart,
And it said, " Though you are captive now in the loud
   pulsing mart,

MANHATTAN

" *Forget not your young days,*
    The dream untarnished still,
  The simple boyhood ways,
    The music of the mill,
And O, the high, green hills of home, crowned with the
  daffodil!

  " *Remember, in your stress,*
    The fragrant flower of youth,
  The ancient loveliness,
    The wise, substantial truth.
The City is a golden lie, a serpent's awful tooth! "

MANHATTAN

II

I love to think of all the true love here,
Pillowed upon the City's throbbing breast;
Though false love stalks through mean or glowing
    streets,
The painted semblance of the dream God gave,
I know the opulent Rose of all the World
Flowers into life with each reviving day,
Is fed by tears from wells of kindliness,
And breathes its deathless perfume on the heart.
I know it lives, here, as in distant dawns
It sprang with fiery wonder when the world
Knew naught of cities; here it thrives the same
As when the first man clasped to his wild breast
The first young passionate woman; here the same
It flourishes and prospers as of old
It leaped to life and rapture every hour,
On endless plains, on hillslopes green with youth,
And in primeval forests burst in flame,
Proud of its lordly loveliness. I know
Its crimson leaves are bruisèd on the stones,
Its petals crushed beneath the tramping feet

MANHATTAN

Of brutal men; but only for a time
It seems to perish; lifted up again
With tenderness, it pours the old fragrance forth,
And from the lips of those who fold it close
Draws the blest sustenance it ever needs.

MANHATTAN

III

At dawn the City stirs. Her body aches
With the mad struggle of the day long dead,
And days before that ground her on their wheel.
She has not slept, for through her veins, the streets,
The tides of life have poured and rushed and beat
As swiftly as they did at Life's high noon.
All through the darkened hours a torrent swept
Down her innumerable thoroughfares,
A raging force that could not be subdued,
And robbed her of her slumber. All night long,
Shattered with pain, she sought to ease her brow
Upon the pillow of darkness—but in vain.
At length, in that strange hour before the light,
I think I heard the tired City sigh,
And heave one breath of utter weariness,
One frantic gasp that might atone for all
The sleep so mercilessly lost to her;
Then, girding all her strength, she rose, and faced
The immemorial sorrow of the day.

I saw the tired City fall in the arms of the Night,
Like a beautiful, weary woman, after the day's delight.

MANHATTAN

And she spake (I heard her whisper when the purple dusk
    came down,
A mantle from high heaven, to cover the teeming town):—

"Mine eyes are heavy with anguish, my bleeding heart is
    oppressed,
For the burden of Life is on me, and I crave a little rest;

"A little ease from the sorrow I bore through the desperate
    day,
A surcease from my struggle and the busy noon's dismay."

But the Night with longing sought her, and crushed her to
    his heart,
And I saw the olden ardor waken and throb and start;

For the Night was her ancient lover, valiant, yet cruel and
    strong,
And he craved a waking woman, on whose lips there lived
    a song;

He gave her wonderful jewels, long strings of glimmering
    pearls,
And her eyes that had been tired gleamed now like a beauti-
    ful girl's.

MANHATTAN

*And he clasped on her throat a necklace that flashed and
    shone like fire;*
O proudly rose the City in imperial attire!

*And she sang (she who was weary) for her glorious lover's
    sake,*
*Though under the song I knew that her heart was like to
    break;*
*She thrilled with the old-time passion, and laughed like a
    little child;*
*When tears came brimming to her eyes, she brushed them
    back—and smiled.*

*Ah! this is the spirit of woman that burns in the City's
    breast—*
*She will turn with a laugh to her lover, forgetting her
    longed-for rest;*

*She will sing when the King commands her, doing his high-
    est will—*
*And thus shall it be till the woman-soul and cities are hushed
    and still.*

MANHATTAN

IV

How punctually God's poor arise to serve
Mammon and Greed! O, day by day they take
Their tragic fate into their hearts again,
And like dumb sheep resume the well-worn paths
That lead to toil. Early the march begins,
Early the solemn phalanx fills the streets—
The giant City's very blood and life!
Look in their eyes—young eyes now old with pain;
Look in their faces lined so soon with care;
Look at their hands, already parchment, bruised
On rough machines that torture while they give
Life's breath—nay, but the shadow of Life's breath!
For this they take their way; for this they spend
The cool, clean hours of morning, and the sweet,
Reluctant hours of honeyed afternoon:—
That in the evening they may fare again
Back to dim homes, through crowds of brothers, lost
In the same awful vortex; stealing there
A broken rest, a brief oblivion
To give them strength to put their armor on
For other days they know will be the same!

MANHATTAN

For this they strive: that they may keep the mouths
Of pallid children fed with food enough
To grow to paler man-·and woman-hood,
And then to follow in the path they knew—
The piteous, narrow, sorrow-stricken way—
Yet wide enough to lead an army on,
Morn after morn, day after desolate day.

MANHATTAN

V

Spring comes to town like some mad girl, who runs
With silver feet upon the Avenue,
And, like Ophelia, in her tresses twines
The first young blossoms—purple violets
And golden daffodils. These are enough—
These fragile handfuls of miraculous bloom—
To make the monster City feel the Spring!
One dash of color on her dun-gray hood,
One flash of yellow near her pallid face,
And she and April are the best of friends—
Benighted town that needs a friend so much!
How she responds to that first soft caress,
And draws the hoyden Spring close to her heart,
And thrills and sings, and for one little time
Forgets the foolish panic of her sons,
Forgets her sordid merchandise and trade,
And lightly trips, while hurdy-gurdies ring—
A wise old crone upon a holiday!

No Spring in any wildwood is like this!
The meadows take young April as they take
The dawn or sunset; gladly, it is true,

MANHATTAN

But without any festival at all.
Why! Spring's as common there as if she came
Each day, each hour! Why make a gala time?
Just let her in, invite her to sit down,
And that's sufficient!

                      But the Spring in town
Meets with a royal welcome that a queen
Might envy all her days. You never knew
Such preparations for one pretty girl!
The vendors herald her with lovely names—
" Lilacs! " and " Tulips! "—yes, and " Mignon-
     ette! "
And " Daffydowndillies! "—who has ever heard
A prettier word upon the human tongue?
And in the parks are spread, in proper rows,
Like Raleigh's coat, for her light feet to tread,
Carpets of green and purple, white and pink,—
Magic designs that flash to sudden life
When April's footfall sounds along the street.

The children hear her first—(they have a way
Of hearing delicate noises), and they fare
To those green islands mercifully set
In the wide City's everlasting sea.

MANHATTAN

They laugh when first the tulips lift their cups
To the blue sky; and when the crocuses
Hold up to heaven their chalices of dew,
They know that Spring has definitely come,
All madness, fragrance, carnival and joy.
Old men renew, for this blithe maiden's sake,
Their vanished youth; and the sad poor come out
To hear her laughter, flinging back at her
Their joyless mirth, repressed and hidden long.
Their tenements are caves of darkness, filled
With horrible air that leads to but one doom.
How wonderful to them the breath of Spring,
The first clear patch of blue above their heads,
The primal tide of warmth through alleys dim
And sick with old remembrance of brief days
Crowded with cold and pain and poverty!
April, your shining feet are needed here
In the dark districts where the City hives
Her palest children, famishing for you.
Speed, Hebe-like, to pour your glowing wine
Not for the gods, but for one God's sick poor,
Whose throats are parched for your delirious cup!

MANHATTAN

VI

What frightful things the City dares to do!
She draws us to her heart, as mothers will,
And nurses us till we are part of her—
Then laughs, and makes our childhood bleak and
        old,
Our youth a lonely flower that starves upon
The iron breast we thought would nourish it.
She leaves us—pitiless Mother!—to control
In helplessness our destiny; forgets
Her children who have come to her, so filled
With beautiful illusions and white dreams.
Unnatural monster!—thus to succor us,
Thus treacherously to catch us in her snare,
To make us love her so we dare not fly
Back to the wind-swept spaces of the West,
Or the cool, valiant mornings of the North,
Or the warm, dripping, singing lanes we left
In the good Southern country.   Utterly
She owns us, as a bondsman owns his slaves,
Exulting in their servitude; and we
Dare not rebel.   Rather, we learn to love

MANHATTAN

The very hand that smites us! And we cling
To the great marble arms enfolding us,
And nestle closer, closer every day!

This is the iron City's awful way—
Not wilfully to crush our bodies down
Beneath her agate heel; but day by day
To choke us with wild loneliness; to drown
Our hearts and hopes—yet never quite to slay.
This is her manner with the sons of men—
To torture us until we bleed with pain;
Yet once her fingers clutch us, futile then
Our hope to wipe away their crimson stain;
Nay, like poor hounds, we kiss her hand again!

She dares to fling us in her frightful tides,
Not knowing whether we can breast the waves;
She hurls us in her seething ocean, there
To fight the perilous currents as we may.
And some go down; and some, on lonely isles
Find shelter that is even worse than death.
They hear the waves—yet dare not face again
Their mighty force; and sundered from the souls
They hoped to make their brothers, they grow old
In the bleak isolation that they know.

MANHATTAN

Like lonesome rocks set in the City's sea,
Are the stone dwellings man himself has reared;
And two poor outcasts, lashed by the same storm
Of bitter circumstance, may live for years
Close to each other—yet a world apart,
Braving the same storms of adversity,
Knowing the same relentless solitude,
Yet fearing to reveal one piteous sign. . . .
What frightful things the City dares to do!

MANHATTAN

VII

A lonely girl sat in a far, high room,
The while below her, like a giant flower,
The city broke in blossom, light by light,
Until, upon this thin branch of the world,
It flaunted its wild yellow and its gold.
She heard the thunder of ten thousand hoofs,
The clang of cars, the bells and motor horns,
The rumble of the Elevated road,
The distant clamor of an ambulance
As swift upon its errand desperate,
It fought its way across a crowded street;
She saw the myriad honeycombs of light,
From towers and high hotels; and far away
The eyes of ferryboats that crawled like worms
Through the deep darkness on their changeless
          course;
And on the far-off shore beyond the town
She saw the faint, sweet lights of little homes
Where waited many a wife and many a child
For the glad coming of the one whose voice
Would crown with rapture the long, tired day.
Far, far below her, in the surging stream,

MANHATTAN

She saw, through tears, hosts of young lovers take
Their happy way along the thoroughfares;
And she could picture, though she could not see,
The laughter in their eyes and on their lips;
And she could guess the wonder in their hearts
As on they swept, like dust upon the flowers
Of the great City's magical bouquet.

Who thought of her, and many like her there,
Lost in the curious system of hotels?—
A quiet guest whom no one seemed to know,
A gentle girl who went her simple way,
Said her " Good-morning " to the passive clerks,
And spent her hours in tragic solitude;
Asked for her slender mail at eight o'clock,
Did her poor scribbling when the mood was on,
And watched the bright procession of the town
When work was not insistent. Day by day,
So went her ordered life. She could endure
The loneliness when all the world was bright
With sunshine, and she had no time to brood
On the green slopes from whence her feet had come.
But O the nights!—the flowering nights of pain,
The lamps of joy that trembled in the streets

MANHATTAN

And threw their bright reflections in her face,
And mocked her when she sat in solitude
In her dim window, awful night on night! . . .
A lonely girl sat in a far, high room.

> *Alone—yet not alone*
> *In this wild whirl and blur;*
> *How vacantly the stone*
> *Stares up at her!*

> *Alone!—but in her heart*
> *Echoes of others' mirth;*
> *Close, close, yet far apart,*
> *O ancient earth!*

> *Alone—with Love so near,*
> *Yet leagues and leagues away;*
> *No wonder that men here*
> *Forget to pray!*

> *Alone! No distance makes*
> *Such solitude as this;*
> *While her heart bleeds and breaks,*
> *Hearken—a kiss!*

MANHATTAN

A lonely man, whose days grew lonelier still,
Fought Life upon the City's battleground,
And turned each sundown to a quiet room,
Where no one waited when his footsteps fell
Along his hotel's echoing corridor.
The Subway, that live worm beneath the ground,
Whirled him at evening to the place he called
His " home "—an empty name that chilled his heart.
The glittering halls that feigned to welcome him,
Killed the last hope of hospitality
By their aggressive grandeur; the paid smiles
Of servile bell-boys irritated him,
And the absurd politeness of the clerks
Seemed but a mockery in this fatuous world.
He was a number—not a name—to them;
He had a room on such and such a floor,
A key that corresponded with the box
Wherein they put his letters—few enough.
He might have died, and little they would care;
He might go out and not come back again.
They'd miss him? Yes, an hour or so, perhaps,
And then, with clock-like regularity,
The wheels of the establishment would turn,
And turn, and turn; and he, who formed one cog

MANHATTAN

In the machinery so deftly oiled,
Would have his place refilled, and—that was all.

One night he saw her in the hall; her eyes
Were young, yet tired, like his; she haunted him,
And all next day, at his hot desk downtown,
He thought of her—that lonely girl whose face
Seemed beautiful and gentle; and he thought
How he would like to have her for his friend.
Yet, if he spoke, he felt she might resent
His brief " Good-evening," and refuse to take
His honest courtesy at its true worth.
Thus, often did he pass her silently. . . .

He learned to watch for her. The weeks went by,
The fleeting months, and though he sometimes saw
Her fragile figure in the dining-room
Or in the hall, he dared not speak to her,
Nor she, of course, to him. . . . Two hungry
          hearts,
Each aching with a nameless emptiness;
Two souls whose very silence must have said
More than a world of speech, a world of tears,
Yet destined to go on their separate ways. . . .
So sped the years for her; and so for him—
A lonely man whose days grew lonelier still.

MANHATTAN

VIII

Sometimes the City, like a woman, hides
Behind a veil, woven of silvery mist;
And sudden darkness plunges every street
In shadow and gloom.   Then comes the purple rain,
Lightly at first, as if afraid to beat
Upon the web of roofs and battlements
That flaunt their challenge to the distant clouds.
A boom sounds in the Harbor.   Jove's loud guns
And all the cavalry of heaven have charged
Upon the solid ramparts of the town.
Bright swords of steel flash in the blackened sky,
And God's great army marches to attack
The bastions standing firm, impregnable,
Strong in their granite beauty everywhere.
Like leaden bullets falls the stinging rain,
And crash on crash the thunder's cannonade
Rolls through the armored City in its might.
O loud the martial language of the storm
Cries out in fury, and the beating hail
Hurls down its fiery shells in awful wrath.
The grim artillery of the Lord of War
Fills with dismay the cowering citizens,

MANHATTAN

Hemmed in like flies who have no sure escape.
Now, now I love your strength, O City! Now
I see your Titan power! Not that you give
Back to the elements what they have given,
But that you bravely face the rough stampede,
And stand your ground, imperishable still!
Not like a rose you droop before the gale,
But like an armored Amazon defend
Your bulwarks, till the last faint shot is fired,
And the white moon and stars come, singing peace.

From heaven's high ramparts sweeping down
The blue battalions stormed the town;
Vast regiments, an endless train,
With slanting bayonets of rain.

With fusillade and open fire
They rushed on turret, dome and spire,
And loudly with a million hoofs
Their cavalry crossed groaning roofs.

Through dripping, tear-swept panes of glass,
I saw the mighty army pass
In silent file, with solemn tramp,
Back to its far, mysterious Camp.

MANHATTAN

IX

They tear them down—the little homes—
They cannot leave them long;
It is as if they robbed the world
Of every little song.

Turrets and towers leap in their place,
When frantic Commerce calls;
And underneath Trade's ruthless hand
Each little homestead falls.

Too soon we lose them—little friends—
Too soon their faces go;
Not Time, but man, has crushed them all,
And laid their beauty low.

Change, change unceasing is the City's cry—
Hew down the trees in every sheltered street,
Build broader avenues and higher towers,
Stretch out into the bright suburban ways,
And snatch the distant villages and towns.
A monster centipede that swiftly stirs,
Manhattan, not content with her domain,
Reaches for far environs greedily.

MANHATTAN

She flings her bridges over waterways,
Magician-like, almost in one brief night,
And hungering for another tiny crumb,
She bores beneath the river a mighty arm,
Until she grasps a bit of countryside,
Seizing it as a spider does a fly.
Her ferryboats, like speeding envoys, keep
Patiently, tirelessly their changeless tracks,
And swing into their slips with punctual pride
Those slips that are their hourly destiny.

When will she cease this terrible desire
For larger power and greater glory? When
Will she repent of her incessant greed,
And, utterly weary of the sense of gain,
Be quite content to say, " My tasks are done;
Now I will rest awhile, for I am tired."

O, never, never will the City sing
The song of labor done; she prospers most
When toiling for the processes of Growth.
Her doom is to be greater, greater still,
Her destiny to lure the country in,
To be a portion of her blood and soul.

MANHATTAN

Her voice is like the ocean's—never hushed;
Her turbulence the waves'—it must go on;
She cannot root up now the seeds long sown,
But, driven hard by that same Fate she made,
She must press forward in the endless race.

MANHATTAN

X

The sweltering Summer brings her furious fires
And lights them on the City's iron hearth.
In the great corridors of streets, the blaze
Leaps high till every pavement trembles with heat,
As August feeds the flame from her deep store.
The rich—because our God is good to them—
Flee to the mountains' shelter or the sea,
Untroubled by the sudden waves of fire;
But the pale army of the poor must stay,
Though on their brows the scorching tongues are laid,
And blistering nights conspire against their rest.
The laborers march to their accustomed toil
In cavernous places where the hot sun pours
His molten beams; and on the asphalt droop
A hundred stricken horses every day.

At sunset, homeward move the dull-eyed throngs;
Some steal their broken slumber in the parks,
Some stretch upon the narrow fire-escapes,
Praying for one soft whisper of the breeze;
And the dim docks that kiss the river's edge

MANHATTAN

Are filled with families gasping for the air.
Here sits a mother with her sickly child,
There aged men pant in the livid heat,
While on the neighboring pier a raucous band
Hurls out its waltz for tireless youth to dance.

Forlorn and ragged refuse of the town,
Poor foreigners who sought our shore with hope,
Now literally upon that shore to dream
A sadly different dream from one now dead,
How my heart breaks for you this breathless night,
Swept here, unhappy derelicts, to stare,
Sleepless, while crawl the hot and tedious hours.

Here in the furnace City, in the humid air they faint,
God's pallid poor, His people, with scarcely space for
breath;
So foul their teeming houses, so full of shame and taint,
They cannot crowd within them for the frightful fear of
Death.

Yet somewhere, Lord, Thine open seas are singing with the
rain,
And somewhere underneath Thy stars the cool waves
crash and beat;

MANHATTAN

Why is it here, and only here, are huddled Death and Pain,
  And here the form of Horror stalks, a menace in the
    street!

The burning flagstones gleam like glass at morning and at
    noon,
  The giant walls shut out the breeze—if any breeze should
    blow;
And high above the smothering town at midnight hangs the
    moon,
  A red medallion in the sky, a monster cameo.

Yet somewhere, God, drenched roses bloom by fountains
    draped with mist,
  In old, lost gardens of the earth made lyrical with rain;
Why is it here a million brows by hungry Death are kissed,
  And here is packed, one Summer night, a whole world's
    fiery pain!

MANHATTAN

XI

Man's greatest miracle is accomplished here.
Steeple and dome he hurls high in the air,
Until, like dreams in marble and in stone,
They lift their wonder to a world amazed.

Behind the poem is the poet's soul;
Behind the canvas throbs the artist's heart;
Behind all music lie unfathomed tones
Known only dimly to one Master mind.
So here, when visions of new beauty rise,
Behind them float the dreams of cities old
Fallen now to silence, with the dust of kings.
Who wrought these granite ghosts, saw more
            than we
May ever see.   He saw pale, tenuous lines
On some age-mellowed shore where cities rose
Proudly as Corinth or imperial Rome;
He saw, through mists of vision, Baghdad leap
To immaterial being, and he sought
To snatch one curve from her elusive domes;
He saw lost Nineveh and Babylon,
And Tyre, and all the golden dreams of Greece,

MANHATTAN

Columns and fanes that cannot be rebuilt,
Ev'n as Shakespearian lines can never sing
Again on any poet's resplendent page.
But the vague Source of these most lovely things
Were his for one high instant; and he caught
Their spirit and their glory for all time.
These are the shadows of far nobler walls,
The wraiths of ancient pomp and glittering days,
Set here by master minds and master souls,
Almost as wonderful as mountains are,
Mysterious as the petals of a flower.

MANHATTAN

XII

On Winter nights, when the clean snow falls down
Like white flowers from the meadows of the sky,
You hear the motors thundering on their way
To fashionable caravanseries,
The theatre or the opera, or the ball.
In bright array the shimmering women sit
Where clinking glasses make their pleasant sound,
And laughter is the gay room's only creed.
Music and lights and beauty—yes, and love—
They make good company on windy nights
When one must somehow manage to forget
The bitterness the season has brought on.
Well, mirth is found here—mirth and revelry;
Let red wine flow, and let the champagne shine
First in its goblet, then in many eyes,
Till the great room seems greater than before,
The music sweeter, women lovelier,
And Love itself, that is the best of all,
Bigger than heaven and earth rolled into one!

This is the way to kill life's youthful hours—

MANHATTAN

These are the places to erase the thought
Of poverty and penury and grief—
Here where mad, jocund conversation hums,
And masks but lure one to imagine all
The tragedy behind such flimsy screens.
It lends an interest to Life to know
That there beside that *grande dame* proudly pale,
Sits a young courtesan whose story is
The common topic of a trivial world.
They would not dine together in *her* home,
They would not sit in the same costly box
At either Opera House; but here—well, this
Alters the case, each one would quickly say;
The harlot gives the *grande dame* something strange
To think of through this tedious dining hour,
And then—who knows?—perhaps the painted girl
Finds very much to ruminate upon
When her quick eyes consider the Lady's face!
How many a flash of understanding whirls
Across this gilded room, one may not know;
But always when I sit in such a place,
And see the comprehension in the eyes
Of men and women of divided spheres,
I think that no such distance separates

MANHATTAN

The half-world and the world as that which flings
The rich and poor immeasurably apart!

When it is time to go they hurry out
To find their motors, and they mark how cold
The wind is; but they seldom toss a coin
To the poor newsboy, shivering near the door.

Out on the jewelled Avenue they see
A priest upon his way to say a prayer
Over a dying man; and for one brief,
Incalculable instant, who may guess
What thoughts are in the merry revellers' minds?
They may have craved the peace he seems to know,
The calm and quiet of his spiritual face;
And to the priest there may have come a wish,
However vague, to snatch one moment's joy
From this apparent happiness and mirth.

They pass the Bread Line—but they do not care,
Flushed now with wine, at ease with all the world;
They hear a street evangelist's faint whine,
And the Salvation Army's simple songs;
They laugh at these—they are not picturesque—
And yet, perhaps, they serve their purposes!

MANHATTAN

So speed these careless groups upon their way,
Poorer than all the mendicants they pass,
And sad in their false joy and harlotry,
Rich only in their prejudice and pride.

MANHATTAN

XIII

I said one day that I would leave the town,
Its madness and pretensions and despair,
And follow once again the ways that lead
To the large wisdom of the wilderness,
And the great mercy of the solitude.
I could not bear the City's ceaseless groans,
Her murmur as of constant weariness,
That echoed and re-echoed like the sound
Of waves upon some memory-haunted shore.
My spirit could not prosper while my heart
Was torn by her continual desire
To scourge her children with her cruel rod.

I fled from her, and looked with sorrow back
Upon this tangled tumult, wondering
Why I had ever loved so utterly
Her smoke-filled miles on miles of ugliness.
And then her awful beauty flashed on me,
As from the lordly Hudson 'neath the moon
I saw her rise in mystery and might,
And then remembered, while my eyes grew dim,
That I had always called this city Home.

MANHATTAN

XIV

There were wild gardens in the spaces where
I sped with eager feet; there were tall trees
Majestically lonely; and blue wastes
Of water, where it seemed no man had been;
There were long shadows in the afternoon,
And velvet evenings when the constant stars
Looked down on me, lost in the perfumed dark;
There were clean rains—baptismal showers that fell
Upon my brow; and mornings shot with threads
Of beauty from the red sun's flaming loom;
And here were dreams, and pauses when it seemed
The world stood still, and Time had ceased to be;
Here energy seemed madness, speech a sin,
And Life one long *Laudate* without end.

I shall not ever know how many days
Had marched away, when first I heard the Sound,
The Quiet Voice that murmured in the trees
And spoke at last so that I understood.
I only know I followed when it called,
I only know I went the way it led,

MANHATTAN

Back to the old, sweet bondage, as a man
Returns to Love, however sad Love be.

When, sick of all the sorrow and distress
  That flourished in the City like foul weeds,
  I sought blue rivers and green, opulent meads,
And leagues of unregarded loneliness
Whereon no foot of man had seemed to press,
  I did not know how great had been my needs,
  How wise the woodland's gospels and her creeds,
How good her faith to one long comfortless.

But in the silence came a Voice to me;
  In every wind it murmured, and I knew
    It would not cease, though far my heart might roam.
  It called me in the sunrise and the dew,
At noon and twilight, sadly, hungrily,
    The jealous City, whispering always—" Home!"

www.ingramcontent.com/pod-product-compliance
Lightning Source LLC
LaVergne TN
LVHW041238080426
835508LV00011B/1272

9 781473 330498